FILIPPOS MANDILARAS

The Battle of Marathon

490 BC

Illustrations
Natalia Kapatsoulia

PAPADOPOULOS PUBLISHING

The Battle of Marathon

Text: Philippos Mandilaras
Illustrations: Natalia Kapatsoulia
Translation: Vaya Kakava

PAPADOPOULOS PUBLISHING
www.epbooks.gr

9, Kapodistriou str., 14452 Metamorfossi Attikis
Tel.: +30 210-2816134
e-mail: info@epbooks.gr

Bookshop
14, Massalias str., 10680 Athens
tel.: +30 210-3615334

ISBN 978-960-569-675-7

There was in the olden days an uninhabited bare plain,
with a village hidden behind the mountain's terrain.
A strip of land ending up to the beach,
where the Persians arrived wishing a lesson to teach.
A handful of Greeks awaited them there,
chased them off to their ships in shame and despair.

Where did one of the most important battles
in history take place?

5th century BC
Persia: an empire vast
as the eye can see,
from the furthest
part of India to
the Aegean Sea.
SARDIS
BABYLON
SUSA
PERSEPOLIS

The Great King rules this land,
with an army invincible, everyone bows at his command.
From his palace of gold he governs the world,
no one dares to resist a king so bold!

Those days in Greece every city was a state,
and alone each one determined its destiny and fate.
In the Agora* all together on friends and enemies agreed,
the leaders heard the public's views and then they'd proceed.

*marketplace

But what are they doing in the marketplace all day?
To me, that's plain stupidity and useless delay!
BLAH BLAH
BLAH
BLAH
BLAH
BLAH
BLAH
BLAH
BLAH
BLAH

A rebellion broke out in Ionia at that time,
an area belonging to the Persian empire in its prime.

Now the people of Ionia were all Greeks.
In Greek they spoke, in Greek they wrote.
So, for assistance to Greece they turned
to have the Persian rule overturned.
But their ambassadors were sadly rejected,
only Eretria & Athens promised to have them defended.

When Darius heard the news he went mad.
Everyone in him had to obey,
but these Greeks, how dare they?

Who are these Athenians sending a fleet?
And those Eretrians, what do they have to do with it?

When they showed him both cities,
fighting side by side...
He laughed: "That's where I'll send
my fleet for a nice boat ride!".

It was clear, on a plan
he had set his mind,
an invasive scheme he had
patiently designed.
In Greece he wanted his army to land
and westwards his empire
to flourish and expand!

And so the Ionian revolt he repressed...

...and prepared his fleet for the campaign to the west.

And quite so, Eretria in six days surrendered,
its women and men all prisoners rendered.

So, the ships set off for the large reed-bed...

beginning
of August
490 BC

...and soon they saw the land of Marathon ahead.

On hearing them in Marathon arrive and land
the Athenian army left Athens and nearby camped.
Right there in Marathon they seeked to arrange the confrontation.
To attack the enemy at the beach, was their calculation.

There's scores of them, they've got cavalry, I'm afraid they'll wipe us out!
If we restrain them in the strait, they won't leave the horses, I've no doubt!
And shall we attack them first, our forces being so scant?
They'll think too little of it, you know they're arrogant!
CALLIMACHUS
Athenian war leader
MILTIADES
Athenian general

Several days they waited training and exercising,
the Persians were tireless, their strength was overwhelming.
Until one hot and boring morning, same as any other,
they saw the Athenians charging their enemy to smother!

Although at first shocked,
the Persians their forces soon regrouped.
Their fierce archers the battle entered,
to point their arrows
to the Greeks intended.
But they were slow to hold back
the Greek soldiers
whose matchless rage against
the foreigners unfolded.

But courage and power
of arms are not enough
to beat an enemy six times
as strong and so tough.
A plan bold and daring you need,
disciplined men
and a general eager to succeed!

This plan, Miltiades sets in motion,
encircling the Persians
in great commotion!

Panicked, they make a run for it, the great Persian hordes,
pursued by the Athenians, waving triumphant swords.

They reach the sea and hurriedly on their ships they go aboard,
wishing to move quickly away from the shore.

Although the battle was lost, we won't give up, at any cost!
Let's head to Athens and conquer it!
Now that in Marathon their men their victory sing, who'll protect their walls from the army of our Great King?

Seeing the ships leave, the Athenians quickly guessed the Persians' plan!

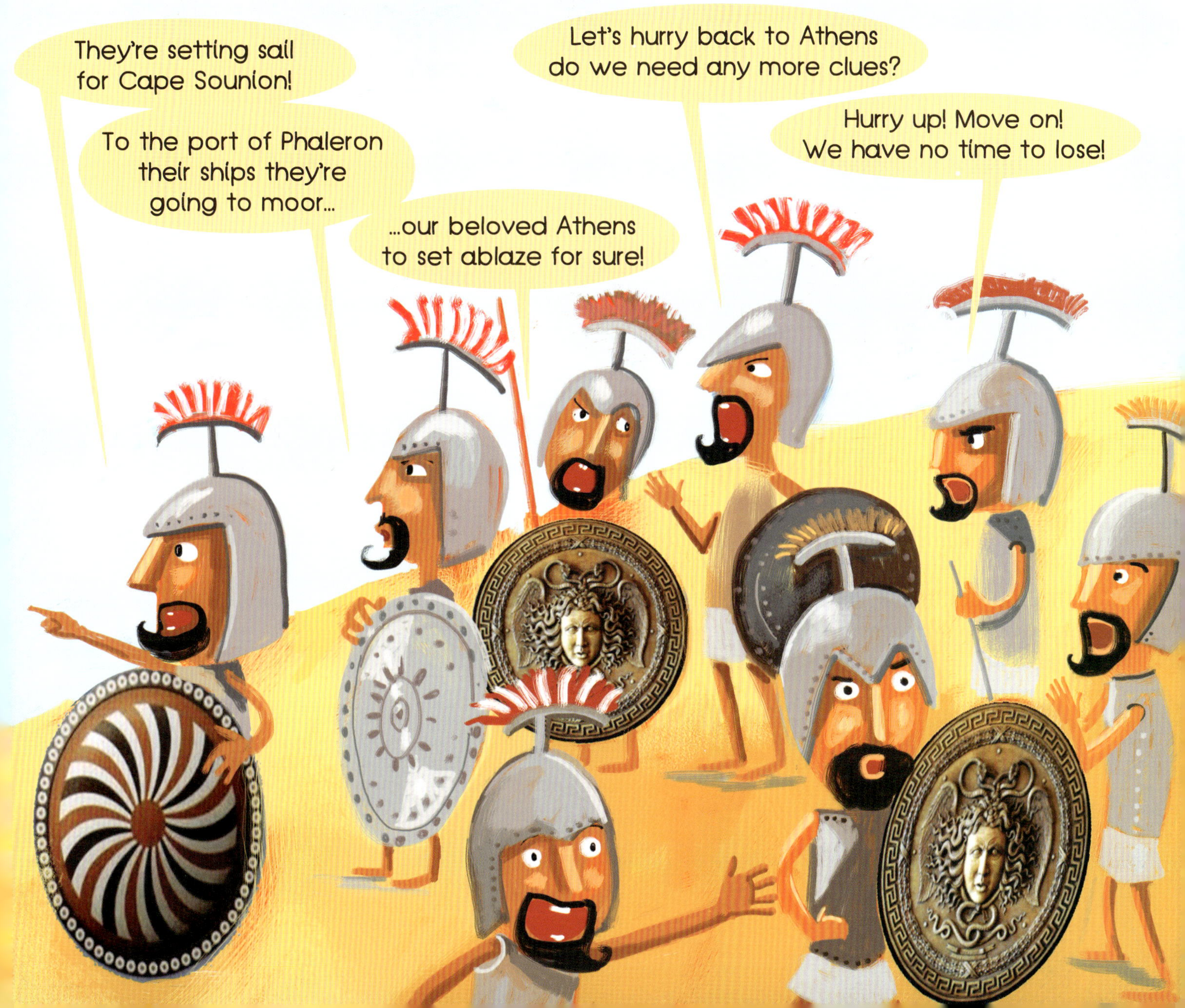

And sure enough, the Persians their ships
to Phaleron steer,
but find Athenian soldiers patrolling
the port with a sneer.
To the Persian generals that's
not a pretty sight,
after being defeated once,
they won't risk another fight!